All About Your Hamster

Contents

D1382031

Introduction

If you own a hamster, or are thinking of getting one, this is the book for you. It gives you all the advice you nee to ensure your pet enjoys a healthy and happy life, as well a providing lots of fascinating facts about the hamster's lifestyle and habits.

First and foremost, you must think about the time, effort and expense that is needed to look after your pet for the whole of its life.

Taking care of a pet – no matter how small – is a big responsibility, and it is something you cannot forget about once the novelty of a new arrival has worn off.

Fortunately, the hamster is a pretty low-maintenance pet that does not make too many demands on its owner.

What is a Rodent?

Hamsters belong to the rodent group of mammals. Like all mammals, they are warm-blooded and have a hairy skin.

Females give birth to live young, and feed them on their own milk. Rodents make up over fifty per cent of all the species of mammals.

They are named after the Latin word rodere, meaning 'to gnaw'.

This is because all rodents have one pair of upper incisor teeth and one pair of lower incisor

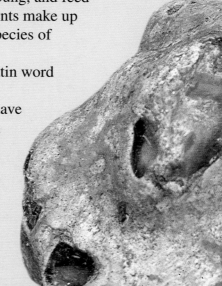

The hamster is an ideal, low–maintenance pet, making few demands on its owner.

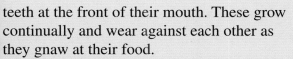

teeth at the front of their mouth. These grow continually and wear against each other as they gnaw at their food.

Rodents range in size from the tiny Old World harvest mouse at around four grammes, to the South American capybara at a massive 40 kg – about ten thousand times heavier!

DID YOU KNOW?

The Roborovski hamster, originating in Northern China, is now becoming popular as a pet. They are even smaller than the other two species of dwarf hamster, but have longer legs and more prominent ears. Their body colour is light chestnut, and they have distinctive white 'eyebrows'.

Hamsters are extremely active when awake, and may travel over 20 kilometres in one night, using their cheek pouches to carry back food to their home burrow, where it is hoarded in underground compartments.

Hamsters are clean and easily tamed.

When we talk of the hamster, most people think of the Golden, or Syrian, hamster. As it is by far the most commonly kept, it is the species that we will concentrate on in this book.

But as we shall see, there are other smaller breeds of hamster that have been introduced to this country more recently, and they have slightly different requirements.

Golden hamsters are clean and easily tamed, although if they do not receive plenty of handling when they are young, they can become anti-social and may inflict a painful bite.

Surprisingly enough, one of the things that they really don't like is other hamsters, and so they have to be kept singly. However, the smaller Russian and Chinese hamsters will live happily in groups if they grow up together. Perhaps one of the main disadvantages of hamsters is their short life span – most will only live a little over two years of age. Losing a pet is always tough – even if you know that life expectancy is short – but at least you can have the satisfaction of knowing that you have given your hamster the best possible love and care.

Handling a Hamster

The correct way to hold a hamster

If hamsters are handled regularly, and gently, from an early age, they will become very tame. They are often asleep during the day, and should not be prodded or startled as they may respond by biting.

A hamster should be picked up in a cupped hand, taking care to hold the animal securely, but not too tightly. Start by gently stroking your hamster when it comes out for food. In time, you can train your pet to respond to a gentle tapping noise that announces that a tasty tidbit is on offer.

Your hamster can also learn to nibble food from your finger, and then sit on the palm of your hand. Once a hamster gets used to being handled, it can be picked up and restrained by grasping the loose skin at the back of the neck with a thumb and finger. Be careful though – hamsters have a tremendous amount of loose skin and can easily turn and nip you, unless you have a firm grip on a very generous piece of scruff.

Golden Hamster

By far the commonest pet is the golden hamster, sometimes called the Syrian hamster – a name that seems preferable, as nowadays golden hamsters are no longer necessarily golden. Over 100 colour varieties have been produced by selective breeding. Single-coloured hamsters are known as 'selfs' and they range from varying shades of golden, through cream, honey, silver-blue, sepia and chocolate, to name but a few. There are also albino strains with no skin pigment at all.

They have a white coat and pink eyes. Marked varieties can be banded, piebald (with white blotches), or mosaic, with a patchwork pattern.

Choice of colour is a matter of personal preference, and, in fact, most hamster owners still favour the original golden colour. There are also varieties with a long coat, which look very attractive, but they do need regular grooming with a toothbrush to keep their coat from matting.

Tortie and white hamster.

A longhair Syrian ham

DID YOU KNOW?

Dwarf hamsters hibernate in the wild, but wake up from time to time for a quick snack.

6

Chinese Hamster

The Chinese hamster, which is found in the wild across much of Eastern Europe and Asia, has been kept as a pet in Britain longer than its golden relative. It is smaller than the golden, and has a greyish-brown coat with a dark stripe down its back.

Chinese hamster.

Dwarf Russian

The Dwarf Russian is, as its name suggests, the smallest of the three species kept as pets. It is usually a buff-brown colour, with a dark brown stripe running from between its eyes, down the back to the base of the tail.

Both smaller species will live in groups, although they are probably happiest if they are reared in pairs. They move pretty fast, and are perhaps a bit shorter-tempered than golden hamsters, so they are not ideal pets for younger children.

The Dwarf Russian is usually more sociable than the Chinese hamster – both with other members of its own species and with humans.

Dwarf Russian hamsters are the most sociable breed, both with other members of their own species and with humans.

Buying a Hamster

DID YOU KNOW?

A hamster's burrow can be very complex, reaching depths of up to one metre.

You can buy a hamster from any good pet store, where experienced staff will be on hand to offer advice.

Alternatively, you may know someone locally who breeds hamsters, and you might be able to find an address of a local hamster club from your library or pet shop.

You may also be able to acquire a hamster from a friend who has bred some. In all instances, look for a hamster that is clean and well-cared-for. In a pet shop, it is a good sign if the staff are knowledge-able and can give you advice when you are making your choice.

Resist the temptation of buying a sickly-looking hamster just because you feel sorry for it – you could end up with a lot of

When choosing your hamster, make sure you go to a well-kept store where the staff can give you advice.

heartache, trouble and expense trying to get it well. It is always best to buy pet hamsters when they are young and readily trainable, aged between five and 12 weeks.

DID YOU KNOW?

Dwarf hamsters communicate among themselves with ultrasonic squeaks that are inaudible to the human ear.

Male or female?

A male hamster.

Dwarf hamsters can be kept as single-sex pairs (that is, two males or two females), so that they

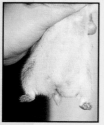

A female hamster.

can keep each other company but will not breed. You will need to enlist the help of an experienced hamster owner who is able to sex hamsters at this young age. Golden hamsters can only be kept singly – and in terms of temperament, it doesn't make any real difference whether you pick a male or a female.

EYES:
bright and clear, without any discharge.

NOSE:
clean and free of discharge.

MOUTH:
clean. Dribbling can be a sign of problems.

BREATHING:
quiet and regular. It should not be laboured.

Healthy hamsters should be inquisitive and active. Remember, they are nocturnal, and so it is best to assess a hamster when it has woken from its daytime sleep. Check for the following signs of good health:

DID YOU KNOW?

In the wild, hamsters shelter from the sun in burrows during the day, coming out at dusk to feed.

BODY CONDITION:
well-covered and rounded. No abnormal swellings.

COAT:
well-groomed, with no sign of soiling or matting.

The Journey Home

Make sure you have suitable housing set up at home before you purchase a new hamster, and carry it home in a small, ventilated box, with some paper shavings for comfort. Do not just pounce on the poor little mite as soon as you get it home – let it settle down alone in its cage with a supply of fresh food and water for a day or two before you start hand-taming.

When it comes to purchasing suitable housing for your hamster you can really let your imagination run riot – if your pocket can stretch that far.

Old-fashioned wire cages are considered pretty boring, and both owners and their pets will get pleasure from one of the colourful range of multi-storey, plastic, modular units that are joined by inter-connecting plastic tubes. These have sleeping areas, restaurants, exercise centres, and even observation towers.

Setting up home: There is a wide variety of hamster equipment to choose from, ranging from wire cages to multi-storey modular units.

But be warned: a unit such as this can end up costing many times more than the hamster. Take care with dwarf hamsters, as the units are generally designed for their larger golden cousins, and they may find the connecting tubes too wide to climb through.

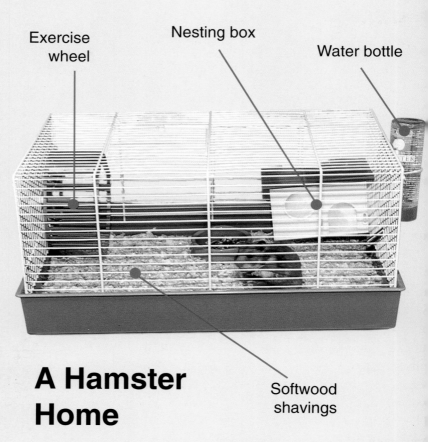

Exercise wheel

Nesting box

Water bottle

Softwood shavings

A Hamster Home

Dwarf hamsters will generally prefer a glass aquarium, with a couple of inches of wood chippings in the bottom. However, the aquarium will need a tight-fitting wire mesh cover to prevent any intrepid escape attempts. If hamsters are kept in a wire cage, it must contain a small nesting box, filled with bedding.

This gives the hamster a warm and secure place to retreat to. Do not place your hamster's home in direct sunlight – this is particularly important with glass aquariums – and try to avoid extremes of temperature.

Bedding

Only approved hamster bedding should be used, as hamsters will often gnaw at and swallow their bedding, and many fibres cannot be digested. This can lead to a blockage of the bowel, which could prove fatal.

Softwood shavings over a base layer of peat are fine, providing the wood that the shavings have been made from has not been chemically treated. Special digestible nesting material is available, which the hamster will take into his sleeping area and arrange to his liking.

Hamsters like to hide their food in corners, and may get upset when it is cleaned away.

The toilet area, which the hamster will select, needs to be cleaned out every day or two, to prevent unpleasant smells and nasty bugs.

Sometimes a hamster can be persuaded to use a jam-jar, positioned on its side. This can be easily removed and washed daily. The whole housing area will need a thorough clean every couple of weeks to remove soiled bedding and hidden food that may be decaying.

A home suitable for dwarf hamsters.

Food should be provided in a clean ceramic bowl (less chewable than a plastic one!), and the hamster should be allowed to help itself to as much as it wants – a lot of it will be hidden anyway.

Play time

A wide range of toys and food treats are available, but they should be selected with care. Wooden blocks with hidey-holes appeal to the tunnelling instincts of hamsters. The use of balls or hamster-dragsters propelled by the hamster running inside, are fine if their use is closely supervised for limited periods. Never leave your hamster unattended in this situation or it could be injured, or become exhausted. Sometimes the cheapest toys are the best - try giving your hamster the cardboard tube from inside a toilet roll. You will be amazed at the fun it will have with the tube, and no harm will be done if it ends up chewed!

Exercise wheel

Because they run about so much in the wild, exercise is essential to a hamster's health and well-being. Most hamsters will get a fair amount of exercise running from one compartment to another in a modular unit, but they should always be provided with a wheel, which gives another form of exercise. However, the wheel must be carefully selected to ensure it is free from sharp edges or holes where small legs could get trapped.

The whole housing area will need to be cleaned every couple of weeks.

On tap!

Hamsters do not generally drink very much, especially if they eat reasonable amounts of succulent foods such as cucumber and lettuce. However, they should always have fresh water available. This is best supplied by a water-bottle with a ball valve underneath so that it can be suspended upside down.

Feeding

Hamsters in the wild eat mostly seeds, some green plant foods, and occasionally grubs and insects. In captivity, their basic diet should be a mix of seeds, grains and nuts. This is available from all good pet shops. It is sold by weight as 'hamster mix', or in pre-packaged form.

Complete pelleted food for rodents is produced commercially for laboratory animals, but can be bought at some pet shops. They contain a complete balance of everything that is needed in the rodent's diet.

Make sure the food is kept clean and dry, and not stored for too long or the vitamin levels will decrease.

In the damp, the food may go off and upset your hamster's digestion. This is especially true of peanuts, that can develop a highly poisonous mould called aflatoxin.

A good-quality 'hamster mix' will provide a well-balanced diet.

Complete foods may supply the basic needs of pet hamsters, but a variety of food provides interest for both the animal and its owner. We all enjoy seeing the pleasure that a special treat may give. Here are some of the things your pet may choose for its picnic hamper:

Hamster hamper

Brazil nut
– great for the teeth.
Apple
– a bit of fruit is appreciated from time to time.
Clover, Dandelion and groundsel – well-washed, fresh from the garden.
Wholemeal toast – but go very easy on the butter.
Carrots – salad vegetables are very popular.
Hard boiled egg – just a little from time to time.

A Syrian hamster with full cheek pouches.

Supplements

If you are giving your hamster a varied diet, or a complete food that has been well made up, there will be no need to add extra vitamins and minerals. If you are concerned that your pet may not be getting enough of these, especially when they are growing, or rearing their young, a tiny pinch of a balanced, small-animal supplement can be sprinkled on to food a couple of times a week.

There ^{are no} ^{vaccinations} that you can give your hamster to prevent diseases, in the way that you can with pet cats and dogs. Fortunately, hamsters are pretty sturdy, low maintenance pets, and as long as you provide them with suitable food and housing as described in this book, problems are rare. A healthy hamster

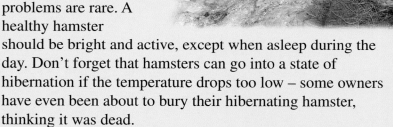

should be bright and active, except when asleep during the day. Don't forget that hamsters can go into a state of hibernation if the temperature drops too low – some owners have even been about to bury their hibernating hamster, thinking it was dead.

A hamster will generally keep its nails in trim by digging and scrabbling around in the cage.

Hamsters' teeth grow all the time, but they normally wear down naturally, providing the hamster has plenty of things to gnaw on. Sometimes the teeth do not grow in proper alignment and they become overgrown.

If this happens, the hamster will show signs of discomfort around the mouth, and the teeth may need regular cutting. If you are concerned about your hamsters' teeth, ask your vet for advice.

Hamsters generally keep their toenails short by digging and scrabbling around the cage, but you should check them from time to time to ensure they do not need clipping, especially if the hamster is elderly.

It is best to get a vet to show you how to clip nails and teeth at first. After that, nail clipping can be carried out at home, using nail-clippers. If you cut a nail too short, it will bleed which will be painful for your hamster.

If your hamster has plenty of things to gnaw on, its teeth will wear down naturally.

DID YOU KNOW?

Hamsters have successfully mated when they were as young as four weeks of age. The ideal age for mating a female is at about two months.

DID YOU KNOW?

The largest recorded litter of pet hamsters was an amazing 26, in Louisiana, USA, in February 1974.

As hamsters are very anti-social, breeding is a complex business and should not be attempted by the novice.

As Syrian hamsters are such anti-social little creatures with regard to others of their own kind, mating and breeding is not straightforward, and should not be attempted by the first-time owner. A female hamster will never allow a male on to her territory, and so the pair will have to be introduced on neutral ground. Even then, fights can easily break out, and it is usually the poor male that gets the worst of it. It is advisable to supervise the meeting with thick gloves at the ready, so that the hamsters can be separated quickly if fighting does start. If the female seems to welcome the advances of the male, they should be left together for about 20 minutes for mating to occur. The male is then removed, as he will play no part in rearing the young. The female should be given plenty of extra bedding and nesting material to construct a nest during pregnancy, and she will start to eat and drink more than normal. A small amount of milk, preferably slightly sour, will help to provide the extra minerals that she needs at this time.

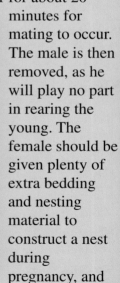

The average litter contains six baby hamsters.

The Litter

The gestation period for a hamster lasts just sixteen days – the shortest of any mammal – and the young are born blind, completely hairless, and unable to do anything other than feed.

An average litter will contain about six youngsters, but over 12 is not unusual. Because the youngsters are so small, the mother almost never has any problems giving birth, a process that will usually take place during the night.

It is important that the nest is not disturbed for the first couple of weeks, as the mother may turn on the young and kill them if she becomes upset.

The babies develop very rapidly, growing fur by the time they are a week old, and beginning to emerge from the nest and take finely chopped solid food after two weeks.

Breeding

They are generally fully weaned by the end of the fourth week and can be separated from their mother at this stage. By six weeks of age they will need to be housed separately, before they begin to fight with each other.

The Dwarf Russian and Chinese hamsters tend to have smaller litters than the golden, averaging around four. Mating is easier, as they will usually live together in mixed sex colonies. The male should not be separated from the female while she is rearing her litter, or he may never be accepted back again.

Unlike the goldens, the males will lend a hand around the house, helping to keep the young warm while Mum is away, and sometimes they will even bring food to the nest. Gestation is a little longer, averaging at 21 days, and the females may re-mate and fall pregnant again within 24 hours of giving birth, thus producing two litters in the space of just six weeks.

It is obvious, therefore, that a colony of dwarf hamsters can multiply at an alarming rate, and unless you know a very large number of people willing to give a good home to a hamster, you will very soon have to separate them into single-sex groups.

Leaving Your Hamster

Hamsters will normally store their food away, so it is okay to leave a hamster unattended for two or three days, so long as there is a good supply of food and water.

Only a small amount of perishable food, such as fruit and green vegetables, should be left. If your hamster is left for longer, you might board it with a vet, a pet shop, or perhaps a breeder.

A hamster is small enough to leave with a friend or relative who is prepared to look after it. If you leave your hamster at home, a daily check for feeding and cleaning by a neighbour should be enough. But leave a contact number for your vet in case problems arise.

DID YOU KNOW?

Hamster is a German word, which originally came from the Slavic word 'chomestoru'.

As hamsters store their food, they can be left unattended for a day or two.

Visiting the Vet

If your hamster is seriously unwell, your veterinary surgeon must be contacted without delay for assistance. In this case, a responsible adult will need to take the hamster to the surgery, and authorise any treatment that may be needed.

A hamster can be cupped gently in two hands to pick it up, and then transferred to a small cardboard or perspex box, with plenty of bedding to keep it warm during the journey. It is most unlikely that a poorly hamster would eat through a cardboard box during the journey, but it should be supervised at all times, just in case.

Most small animal veterinary practices see a large number of small mammals, and so they are very willing and able to treat them. These days, it is even possible to anaesthetise hamsters to carry out surgical operations, such as tumour removal, or even amputation of a badly damaged limb – although the risks are greater than for a cat or a dog undergoing a similar procedure.

DID YOU KNOW?

Earlier this century, golden hamsters were thought to be extinct. Every hamster in captivity today is descended from a single family of hamsters discovered in Syria in 1932.

A well cared-for hamster should suffer few major health problems.

First Aid

The most important care for a sick or injured hamster is to keep it warm and administer fluids to try and prevent dehydration, which can occur quite quickly. A dropper or a small syringe is ideal for administering solutions, but do not use excessive force, and remember that they can do more harm than good if fluids are inhaled.

Commercial rehydration powders that are made up with water can be purchased from a vet or a pharmacist, but a hamster will only take a few drops at a time. Alternatively, you can use boiled tap-water that has been allowed to cool, adding a heaped tablespoonful of glucose powder and a level teaspoonful of salt per pint. Small wounds can be gently flushed with warm water and treated with a mild antiseptic, but any major injuries will require veterinary attention.

The hamster is a very inquisitive creature, and, unfortunately, this can lead to accidents. It is not uncommon for an exploring hamster to fall off a high surface. If this happens, place the hamster in its nest to recover from the shock. If the hamster is not visibly improving within an hour, it may have broken some bones or suffered internal injuries.

Common Ailments

Abscesses

These may develop on the body as a result of injuries on sharp objects, or from fighting when more than one hamster is kept together. Abscesses may also develop within the mouth as a result of tooth problems, or from unsuitable food building up in the cheek pouches.

They consist of raw, smelly discharging areas that have become infected by bacteria. Antibiotic treatment from a vet will usually be required. If the hamster will tolerate it, regular bathing of the affected areas with a solution of one teaspoonful of salt in a pint of warm water will be helpful.

Constipation

This may occur in young hamsters just before they are weaned if they do not have access to fluids other than mother's milk. It can also occur in older animals if they swallow the wrong sort of bedding material, such as cotton-wool. The hamster develops a swollen tummy and goes off its food. Extra green vegetables and fruit usually cures the problem.

Skin Problems

Mature male hamsters often develop dark spots, covered by coarse hair, either side of their body over the hips. This is not abnormal – it is due to scent gland development in these areas. Sometimes the glands become sore and trouble the hamster, and may need treatment with an ointment to reduce the irritation.

Hair loss around the ears, on the rear, and underneath the tummy is also common in older hamsters.

Infectious skin problems are not common in hamsters kept as pets, because they generally have very little opportunity to come into contact with other hamsters. It is possible for them to suffer from ringworm, a fungus that grows on the hairs, which can also cause skin problems in humans and other animals.

Ear Mites ●────────────────

These tiny parasites live down the ear canal and sometimes on the skin around the head, causing crusting and itchiness. Putting ear drops into a tiny hamster's ears is pretty well impossible, but an injection can be given to kill the mites. Ear mites are not contagious to other animals.

Common Ailments

Hamsters can also be affected by demodectic mange mites, which are long, thin parasites that live in the root follicles of the hairs, causing patches of baldness.

Eye Problems

Conjunctivitis is not uncommon in hamsters. This condition can cause sore eyes, and the eyelids may even gum up and stick together, trapping the discharge underneath them.

It can be sparked off by a more generalised problem, such as a respiratory infection, or by irritation of the eyes by dust particles. The eyes should be bathed in a saline solution of one teaspoonful of salt to a pint of warm, boiled water, and, if necessary, the eyelids should be gently prised open. A veterinary surgeon will be able to prescribe an antibiotic ointment to treat the problem.

Poisoning

Hamsters are quite sensitive to poisoning, particularly because they spend a lot of time grooming and will lick off any substances that get on to their coat. Do not use aerosol sprays in the room where the hamster lives without checking first that they are non-toxic to animals.

Wet Tail

So-named because of the wetness and staining that occurs around the tail in affected hamsters. It is usually due to diarrhoea caused by an infection of lower part of the bowel, but in female hamsters it can also be due to a womb infection. Affected animals will be hunched up, listless and uninterested in food, and the diarrhoea can quickly spread between hamsters in a colony. The outlook for affected animals is not good, but some animals do recover with prompt treatment.

Breathing Problems

Snuffling due to upper airway infections are quite common, especially if the hamster is kept in damp or draughty conditions. Sometimes this can lead on to pneumonia, an infection on the lungs, which is also common in older hamsters that have a low resistance to disease. This is very often fatal.

Cancer

This is a very common condition in older hamsters, occurring in many different sites around the body. It can only rarely be treated by surgery.